Table of Contents

Teaching Strategies and Activities

Transparencies

P9-AQL-342

GLENCOE

WORLD HISTORY

Cause-and-Effect
Transparencies,
Strategies, and Activities

New York, New York   Columbus, Ohio   Chicago, Illinois   Woodland Hills, California

Flowering of Civilizations: Causes and Effects

Objective
Students will identify causes and effects of the flowering of civilizations.

Strategy
Remind students that major civilizations arose and flourished around the world in the period from prehistory to A.D. 500. Emphasize that although the civilizations that form the focus of the unit developed in different parts of the world and had unique characteristics, common factors contributed to their rise and success. Also point out that each left a legacy of achievements and ideas to civilizations that followed.

Analyzing Information
On a globe or world map, have students locate the civilizations described in this unit. As each civilization is located, call on students to provide a brief synopsis of the development of the civilization. On the board, write the name of the civilization and the factors that supported the flowering of each civilization. Then hold a brainstorming session in which students identify achievements of each civilization. Record their ideas on the board in a chart under the headings *Civilization* and *Achievements*.

When students have finished brainstorming, draw their attention to the items in the chart. Ask them to categorize each achievement under one of the following headings, thus creating a second chart: *Politics, Religion and Philosophy, Science, Arts and Literature*. As they do, record their responses in the chart.

Help students generalize about the causes and effects of the flowering of civilizations on the basis of the two charts. Ask:

Why did these civilizations flower?

What did they leave behind?

Explain to students that their general answer to the *why* question will identify causes of the flowering of civilizations and that their general response to the *what* question will identify effects.

Display the transparency. Ask students:

- **Which items in the diagram explain why major civilizations arose in different parts of the world?** (*political stability, development of religion and philosophy, trade and expansion, interest in arts and sciences*)

- **How did the major civilizations influence the world?** (*They contributed forms and concepts of government; religious and philosophical movements; scientific theories and inventions; classical styles of art, architecture, and literature.*)

- **Which factor do you think is absolutely essential to the flowering of civilizations? Explain.** (*Answers will vary but may include interest in arts and sciences, because it inspires achievements in those areas that make a civilization unique or a leader; political stability, because people cannot be creative and productive in a shaky political situation.*)

- **How has the flowering of early civilizations affected our lives?** (*Answers will vary but may include in our country's democratic form of government; religions and philosophies followed by people today began in ancient times when major civilizations flourished; early scientific theories and inventions such as the concept of zero and Arabic numerals are still in use; classical styles serve as models for contemporary artwork, buildings, and literature.*)

Go a Step Further
Distribute the Cause-and-Effect Transparency 1 Activity. Instruct students to refer to the transparency to answer the questions.

Flowering of Civilizations: Causes and Effects

DIRECTIONS: **Understanding Causes and Effects** Examine the cause-and-effect diagram. Also think about what you learned in this unit. Then answer the following questions.

1. What are the four main causes of the flowering of civilizations? _____

    _____

2. What effects of the flowering of ancient civilizations does the diagram show? _____

    _____

    _____

3. What do most historians equate with the rise of civilizations? _____

    _____

4. How did the *Pax Romana* contribute to the flowering of civilization in Rome? _____

    _____

    _____

5. How does trade contribute to the development of civilization? _____

    _____

6. How did expansion under Alexander the Great affect Greek civilization? _____

    _____

    _____

7. What major religions developed in India? _____

8. What major philosophies appeared in early China? _____

    _____

9. Which early civilization's political system is considered the basis of our own democratic

    government? _____

10. In what ways have different cultures contacted one another? What are the general results of

    these contacts? _____

    _____

11. Why have the religious and philosophical movements begun in ancient times survived to

    this day? _____

    _____

Regional Civilizations: Causes and Effects

Objective
Students will identify causes and effects of contact between cultures in the period 400–1500.

Strategy
Remind students that during the period 400–1500, people from many different cultures came into contact with one another. Prompt students to identify the different societies that developed at this time. Discuss the contacts and influence of each.

Analyzing Information
To emphasize the global occurrence of cultural diffusion, list the societies students name and call on students to locate them on a world map or globe. Then make a web diagram centered on each society that offers a graphic illustration of its contacts and influence.

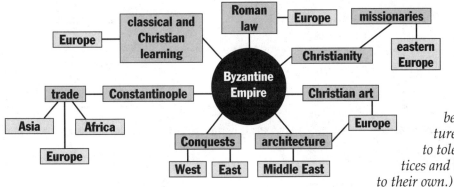

Have students make generalizations about contacts between cultures on the basis of the diagrams. Ask:

How did different cultures come into contact?

What happened as a result of these contacts?

Explain that the general answer to the *how* question will identify causes of contact between cultures and that the general response to the *what* question will identify effects.

Display the transparency. Ask students:

- **How did cultures come into contact in this period?** *(through religious missions, trade, and conquest)*

- **What did contact between cultures lead to?** *(spread of religions, new ways of life, tolerance of others, expansion of trade, exchange of ideas, conflict)*

- **How can trade be both a cause and an effect of contact between cultures?** *(Trade offers an opportunity for different cultures to meet and exchange ideas and goods; if such meetings are positive and profitable, different cultures might increase trade with each other.)*

- **How would you account for the fact that contact between cultures results in both conflict and tolerance?** *(Conflict often develops when cultures come into contact in war or try to force their ideas and beliefs on each other; cultures can choose, however, to tolerate each other's practices and beliefs while holding on to their own.)*

- **Why do you think a crossroads is used to show contacts between cultures?** *(because a crossroads is where roads from different places come together)*

Go a Step Further
Distribute the Cause-and-Effect Transparency 2 Activity. Instruct students to refer to the transparency to answer the questions.

Regional Civilizations: Causes and Effects

DIRECTIONS: Understanding Causes and Effects Examine the cause-and-effect diagram. Also think about what you learned in this unit. Then answer the following questions.

1. What were the causes of contact between cultures, according to the diagram? _____
_____

2. What were the effects of contact between cultures? _____
_____
_____

3. Which culture spread its religion through conquest? _____

4. Under which cause would the Crusades be classified? Why? _____
_____

5. What were three important trading centers of the period? _____
_____

6. Where did Muslim scientists get some of the ideas on which they based their work in mathematics, astronomy, chemistry, and medicine? _____
_____

7. What religions spread over wide areas during this period? _____
_____

8. Along what route did ideas and goods pass between China and cultures to the west?
_____

9. How did Mesoamerican and South American cultures such as the Mayan, Aztec, and Incan come into contact with other cultures? _____

10. What people created the largest land empire in history by conquering China? Who led this conquest? _____
_____

11. What people carried on most of the trade across the Sahara? _____
_____

The Renaissance: Causes and Effects

Objective
Students will identify causes and effects of the Renaissance.

Strategy
Explain that while civilizations in Asia were reaching peaks of cultural achievement, Europeans were forming a new outlook on the world. Remind students that this time of new directions in Europe was called the Renaissance. Point out that the period of cultural rebirth in Europe known as the Renaissance was in some ways a continuation of the Middle Ages but also marked the beginning of the modern era. Trace the development of the Renaissance from Italy into northern Europe and discuss its impact on the world beyond Europe.

Analyzing Information
Encourage students to identify aspects of the Renaissance by creating a cluster around the concept. Write the word *Renaissance* in the center of the board or on a blank transparency. Then prompt students to recall what they have learned about the Renaissance. As students brainstorm and make associations, write their ideas in a cluster around the word *Renaissance*.

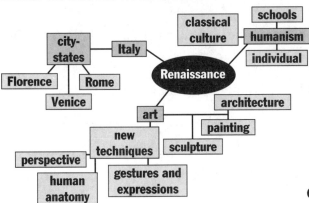

Use the completed cluster as a springboard for discussion of the causes and effects of the Renaissance. Ask:

Why did Europe experience a cultural awakening?

What happened as a result of the Renaissance?

Have students identify information included in the cluster that might answer these questions. Explain that the *why* question will help them identify causes of the Renaissance and that the *what* question will help them identify effects.

Display the transparency. Ask students:

- **What led to the Renaissance?** (*humanism; secularism; questioning of ideas, traditions, and institutions*)

- **Where did the Renaissance lead?** (*religious reforms, interest in social issues, new forms of literature, artistic achievements, exploration and colonization*)

- **What is humanism, and how did it mark a break with ideas of the Middle Ages?** (*interest in the classics; the classical idea of seeking fulfillment in daily life stood in contrast to the medieval idea that people should expect little comfort from life on earth; the classics also promoted the idea of the dignity and worth of each individual*)

- **What is secularism, and how did it differ from attitudes during the Middle Ages?** (*focus on the worldly, or nonreligious; religion was the main focus during the Middle Ages, and most creative endeavors had religious subjects*)

- **Why do you think the Renaissance is shown as a rising sun?** (*Answers will vary but may include that the Renaissance represented the dawn of a new day for Europe.*)

Go a Step Further
Distribute the Cause-and-Effect Transparency 3 Activity. Instruct students to refer to the transparency to answer the questions.

Cause-and-Effect Transparency 3 Activity

The Renaissance: Causes and Effects

DIRECTIONS: Understanding Causes and Effects Examine the cause-and-effect diagram. Also think about what you learned in this unit. Then answer the following questions.

1. What were the causes of the Renaissance, according to the diagram? _____

   _____

2. What effects of the Renaissance does the diagram show? _____

   _____

3. What specific causes of the Italian Renaissance would you add to the diagram? _____

   _____

4. How are humanism and the questioning of ideas, traditions, and institutions connected?

   _____

   _____

5. How did humanism affect literature? _____

   _____

6. How was Renaissance art more secular than art of the Middle Ages? _____

   _____

   _____

7. What religious reforms came about during the Renaissance? _____

   _____

8. What northern Europeans urged people to question the institution of the Catholic Church?

   _____

9. What was the Council of Trent, and where does it belong in the diagram? _____

   _____

10. What literary works and artistic achievements could be called characteristic of the

    Renaissance in Italy, in France, in northern Europe, and in England? _____

    _____

    _____

11. What are the primary factors that motivated Europeans to explore new continents? _____

    _____

The Industrial Revolution: Causes and Effects

Objective
Students will identify causes and effects of the Industrial Revolution.

Strategy
Remind students that the 1800s were a time of dramatic changes. Recall that technological advances brought social and cultural changes: new technologies changed ways of working, and new ways of working led to changes in people's ways of living and thinking. Observe that these tremendous changes constituted a revolution, or a complete transformation of life.

Compare and contrast living and working conditions in Europe before the Industrial Revolution with conditions during the age of industry.

Analyzing Information
Use the summary provided in the chart below to open discussion of the causes and effects of the Industrial Revolution.

Before the 1800s	After the 1800s
Lived in rural villages	Lived in cities
Farmed small tracts of land	Worked in factories
Made things their families needed	Manufactured goods on a large scale

Ask students to consider the following questions:

Why did living and working conditions change?

What happened as a result of this transformation?

Explain that the *why* question will help them identify causes of the Industrial Revolution and the *what* question will help them identify effects.

Display the transparency. Ask:

- **Which items in the diagram explain why living and working conditions changed?** *(population growth, exploitation of natural resources, technological advances)*

- **What did the Industrial Revolution lead to?** *(use of new sources of power, invention of new technologies, search for raw materials and new markets, rise of middle class, birth of big business, growth of cities, development of new philosophies)*

- **How would you describe the relationship between industrialization and the growth of cities?** *(The building of factories near available natural resources drew the new workers from the countryside and overseas, leading to large concentrations of population.)*

- **How can new technology be both a cause and an effect of industrialization?** *(New technology was necessary to help industry to grow, and once industry grew, new technology was needed to help it continue to develop.)*

- **How does the artwork on the transparency symbolize the effects of the Industrial Revolution?** *(The events affected each other as much as one gear causes another gear to move.)*

Go a Step Further

Duplicate and distribute the Cause-and-Effect Transparency 4 Activity. Instruct students to refer to the transparency to answer the questions.

The Industrial Revolution: Causes and Effects

DIRECTIONS: **Understanding Causes and Effects** Examine the cause-and-effect diagram. Also think about what you learned in this unit. Then answer the following questions.

1. According to the diagram, what were the three main causes of the Industrial Revolution?
   _____

2. What direct effects of industrialization does the diagram show? _____
   _____

   _____

3. What natural resources did Great Britain use to develop industry? _____
   _____

4. What were some technological advances that brought about the Industrial Revolution?
   _____

5. What changes in agriculture contributed to a growth in population? _____
   _____

6. How did these changes in agriculture increase the labor supply? _____
   _____

7. What new source of power transformed industry and improved transportation? _____
   _____

8. What inventions represented advances in communications? _____
   _____

9. Where did industrial nations look for raw materials and new markets? _____
   _____

10. Why did big business develop as a result of the Industrial Revolution? _____
    _____

11. How did the rise of the middle class lead to democratic reforms? _____
    _____

12. How are industrialization and the growth of cities connected? _____
    _____

13. What new philosophies called for social reforms? _____

World Wars: Causes and Effects

Objective
Students will identify causes and effects of the two World Wars.

Strategy
Remind students that in the first half of the twentieth century, two destructive wars engulfed the world. Point out that nationalism and imperialism influenced relations among countries, causing nations to compete and clash with each other. Note that these international tensions ultimately led to war. Conclude by observing that both wars changed world affairs and people's ways of life.

Analyzing Information
To help students differentiate between the two World Wars, create a concept map for each that organizes essential facts about it.

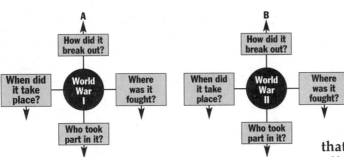

Use the concept maps to prompt students to recall what they have learned about World War I and World War II. As students provide information about each war, add facts to the appropriate concept map. After completing the concept maps, note that the maps do not include *why* or *what* questions about the wars. Then ask:

Why did nations engage in World War I? World War II?

What happened as a result of World War I? World War II?

Explain to students that the *why* questions will help them identify causes of the two wars and the *what* questions will help them identify effects.

Display the transparency. Ask students:

- **Which items in the diagram explain why the nations of the world became engulfed in World War I?** (*economic competition, nationalism, militarism, alliances*) **In World War II?** (*resentment, economic suffering, social chaos, nationalism, rise of dictatorships, aggressive expansion*)

- **What were the outcomes of World War I?** (*end of old order, political instability, disillusionment, resentment, economic suffering, social chaos, nationalism, rise of dictatorships, aggressive expansion*) **Of World War II?** (*shift in balance of power, economic mobilization, creation of new nations, beginning of the Cold War*)

- **Why might industrialization be called a cause of World War I?** (*because as Western nations industrialized, each sought the most favorable conditions for economic growth, which led to intense economic competition among nations*)

- **How do you account for the fact that nationalism is both a cause and an effect of world war?** (*because nationalism can be an extremely divisive force, separating nations instead of bringing them together, it often leads to conflict; after the conflict is over, bitterness or humiliation often rekindles nationalist feelings*)

- **What happened to the superpowers that emerged after World War II?** (*The Soviet Union no longer exists; the United States of America remains a superpower.*)

Go a Step Further
Duplicate and distribute the Cause-and-Effect Transparency 5 Activity. Instruct students to refer to the transparency to answer the questions.

Cause-and-Effect Transparency 5 Activity

World Wars: Causes and Effects

DIRECTIONS: Understanding Causes and Effects Examine the cause-and-effect diagram. Also think about what you learned in this unit. Then answer the following questions.

1. What were the causes of World War I, according to the diagram? _____
   _____

2. What effects of World War I are shown? _____
   _____

3. What effects of World War I were causes of World War II? _____
   _____

4. What were the effects of World War II, according to the diagram? _____
   _____

5. Where in Europe were nationalist movements especially strong before World War I?
   _____

6. What alliances threatened the peace of the European continent before World War I?
   _____

7. Why did Germany resent the terms of the Treaty of Versailles? _____
   _____

8. Where did dictatorships arise following World War I? _____

9. What was the primary goal of the authoritarian governments that arose after World War I?
   _____

10. What nations practiced a policy of aggressive expansion that aggravated tensions before
    World War II? _____

11. Where did nationalist and independence movements grow between the two World Wars?
    _____

12. Why did President Truman decide to use atomic bombs against Japan? _____
    _____

13. What was the origin of the Cold War? _____
    _____

Glencoe World History

Global Interdependence: Causes and Effects

Objective
Students will identify causes and effects of global interdependence.

Strategy
Remind students that international tensions continued after World War II. Point out that the United States and the Soviet Union emerged from the war as superpowers and became locked in a struggle for global influence. Prompt students to recall that this face-off became known as the Cold War. Review the effects of the Cold War and the events that led to its end. Conclude by observing that the end of the Cold War, which was signaled by the collapse of the Soviet Union and the emergence of new republics, opened up a new era in which global interdependence, though threatened by conflicts, remains the only hope for the world's future.

Analyzing Information
Use a cause-and-effect diagram as a visual aid to review the Cold War period.

End of wartime alliances → Emergence of superpowers → Cold War → division of Europe, aid for weaker nations, founding of Warsaw Pact and NATO, armed conflicts, use of propaganda, arms race, fear and reaction at home, widespread espionage

Examine the diagram and call on students to cite specific examples of the effects of the Cold War. After considering the end of the Cold War, refocus the discussion on the present and future. To provoke thought about the new era of global interdependence in which students live, ask:

Why have the nations of the world become more interdependent?

What will happen as a result of their interdependence?

Note that the *why* question will help students identify causes of global interdependence and the *what* question will help them identify effects.

Display the transparency. Ask students:

- **Which items in the diagram explain why nations have become more interdependent?** *(advances in science and technology, common economic interests, concern for environment, desire for peace and security)*

- **What might global interdependence lead to?** *(sharing of resources, responsibility for environment, peaceful resolution of conflict, acceptance of differences, universal human rights)*

- **What has caused hope for a new era of global cooperation to fade since the end of the Cold War?** *(Answers will vary but may include ethnic rivalries that have led to bloody conflict.)*

- **Which effects of global interdependence are some of the world's people already beginning to enjoy?** *(sharing of resources, responsibility for environment, peaceful resolution of conflict, acceptance of differences)*

- **Which effect of global interdependence has not yet been experienced?** *(universal human rights)*

Go a Step Further
Duplicate and distribute the Cause-and-Effect Transparency 6 Activity. Instruct students to refer to the transparency to answer the questions.

Global Interdependence: Causes and Effects

DIRECTIONS: Understanding Causes and Effects Examine the cause-and-effect diagram. Also think about what you learned in this unit. Then answer the following questions.

1. What are the causes of global interdependence according to the diagram? _____
_____

2. What effects of global interdependence does the diagram show? _____
_____

3. What advances in communications have helped to link people around the world?
_____

4. What countries tried unsuccessfully to introduce drastic reforms?
_____

5. In what parts of the world are many people still struggling to meet their basic needs?
_____

6. What factors contribute to world hunger? _____
_____

7. What concerns about the environment do nations share? _____
_____

8. Why is the sharing of the world's resources more critical than ever? _____
_____

9. What are some possible causes of recent acts of terrorism in the world? _____
_____

10. Where have attempts been made to resolve differences peacefully? Where has peaceful resolution of conflict proved more difficult? _____

11. How can global interdependence lead to the acceptance of differences? _____
_____

12. How can the world's people do their part to achieve universal human rights?
_____

Glencoe World History

UNIT 1
Activity 1, p. 2

1. political stability, development of religion and philosophy, trade and expansion, interest in arts and sciences
2. forms and concepts of government; religious and philosophical movements; scientific theories and inventions; classical styles of art, architecture, and literature
3. rise of cities
4. It was a time of peace and prosperity during which the Romans achieved a great deal in the areas of law, public works, architecture, and literature.
5. In addition to goods, people exchanged ideas and beliefs, which they used in developing their civilization.
6. Greek culture spread and mixed with Middle Eastern culture, and a new civilization, known as Hellenistic civilization, flowered outside of Greece in places such as Alexandria in Egypt.
7. Hinduism and Buddhism
8. Confucianism and Daosim
9. Greece
10. Answers will vary but may include the following: Contact through trade, war, and exploration has resulted in the spread of ideas, goods, and customs.
11. because their ideas, beliefs, messages, and ways still appeal to people and have meaning for them

UNIT 2
Activity 2, p. 4

1. religious missions, trade, conquest
2. spread of religions, new ways of life, tolerance of others, expansion of trade, exchange of ideas, conflict
3. Islamic culture
4. religious mission; because the crusaders set out to recover the Holy Land from the Muslims
5. Answers will vary but may include the following: Constantinople, Venice, Baghdad, Cairo.
6. Greece and India
7. Christianity, Islam, Confucianism, and Buddhism
8. Silk Road

9. through conquest
10. Mongols; Genghis Khan
11. the Berbers

UNIT 3
Activity 3, p. 6

1. humanism; secularism; questioning of ideas, traditions, and institutions
2. religious reforms, interest in social issues, new forms of literature, artistic achievements, exploration and colonization
3. thriving towns, leaders interested in art and intellectual pursuits
4. Humanist scholars were independent thinkers and began to challenge long-accepted ideas, traditions, and institutions.
5. It inspired writing about daily life and human feelings and led to writing in the language of everyday speech instead of Latin, making literature accessible to more people and inspiring regional pride.
6. Renaissance artists used perspective and studies of human anatomy to create realistic portrayals of the world around them. They also went beyond realism to create depictions of perfection in nature and human beauty.
7. a split in the Catholic Church (the Protestant Reformation) that produced a new form of Christianity known as Protestantism; divisions within the Protestant movement; and the elimination of abuses, clarification of theology, and reestablishment of the pope's authority within the Catholic Church (Catholic Reformation or Counter-Reformation)
8. Desiderius Erasmus, Martin Luther, Huldrych Zwingli, John Calvin
9. a gathering of bishops at Trent, Italy, to define the official doctrine of the Catholic Church; it is an example of "Religious Reforms"
10. Answers will vary but may include the following: Italy: Baldassare Castiglione's *Book of the Courtier*, Dante's *Divine Comedy*, Michaelangelo's paintings in the Sistine Chapel, sonnets of Petrarch, Leonardo da Vinci's *Last Supper*; France: Christine de Pizan's *The Book of the City of Ladies*; northern Europe: paintings by Jan van Eyck; England: plays of William Shakespeare.
11. the desire for trade and the promise of riches, religious zeal, increased economic resources

that provided funding for exploratory journeys, improved maritime technologies needed for long journeys

UNIT 4
Activity 4, p. 8
1. population growth, exploitation of natural resources, technological advances
2. use of new sources of power, invention of new technologies, search for additional raw materials and new markets, rise of middle class, birth of big business, growth of cities, development of new philosophies
3. water (harbors, network of rivers, water power), iron ore, coal
4. machines such as the "flying shuttle," spinning jenny, water-powered loom, steam engine
5. more farmland, an improved climate, and new vegetables such as the potato
6. general population increased because improvements in farming led to an increased availability of food, and people were healthier and lived longer
7. steam
8. telephone, wireless telegraph
9. Africa, Asia, Latin America
10. The increase in production resulted in greater profits, which could be used for expansion of business.
11. People in the middle class demanded greater representation in government.
12. Many factories were located in or near cities, and workers relocated in cities to live close to their work.
13. socialism, Marxism

UNIT 5
Activity 5, p. 10
1. economic competition, nationalism, militarism, alliances
2. end of old order, political instability, disillusionment, resentment, economic suffering, social chaos, nationalism, rise of dictatorships, aggressive expansion
3. resentment, economic suffering, social chaos, nationalism, rise of dictatorships, aggressive expansion
4. shift in balance of power, economic mobilization, creation of new nations, beginning of the Cold War

5. Germany, France, the Slavic territories of Austria-Hungary
6. Triple Alliance: Austria-Hungary, Germany, Italy; Triple Entente: France, Russia, Great Britain
7. because the treaty reduced the size of its army and its territory at home and abroad; in addition, Germany had to pay reparations to other countries for damage and costs incurred during the war.
8. Italy, Germany, Soviet Union
9. to preserve the existing social order and to better economic conditions
10. Japan (invasion of China), Italy (conquest of Ethiopia), Germany (occupation of the Rhineland, annexation of Austria, etc.)
11. Asia, Africa, Latin America
12. to avoid human casualties that would have resulted from a land invasion
13. differences between the democratic ideals of the United States and the communist ideals of the Soviet Union

UNIT 6
Activity 6, p. 12
1. advances in science and technology, common economic interests, concern for environment, desire for peace and security
2. sharing of resources, responsibility for environment, peaceful resolution of conflict, acceptance of differences, universal human rights
3. satellite communications, satellite dishes, Internet computer network
4. Answers will vary but may include the following: People's Republic of China, Iran, and the Soviet Union.
5. developing nations of Asia, Africa, and Latin America
6. Answers will vary but may include the following: poor soil, increasing population size, natural disasters, war, economic factors, and environmental degradation.
7. harm to wildlife from pesticides, deforestation, acid rain, chemical waste, global warming
8. because the world's population is increasing rapidly, and there is a huge demand for resources, especially in developed nations
9. religious and cultural differences, poverty, ignorance, territorial disputes

10. South Africa, the Balkans, the Middle East (Israel); answers will vary but may include the following: Bosnia-Herzegovina and Afghanistan.

11. When people need one another to live, they must be willing to live with one another no matter what their differences.

12. Answers will vary but may include the following: on a small scale at home or in the community, by acting globally.